D1443204

LEGO DC COMICS SUPER HEROES

AMAZING BATTLES!

Written by
Rosie Peet

Editorial Assistant Rosie Peet
Senior Editor Hannah Dolan
Designer Sandra Perry
Managing Editors Elizabeth Dowsett, Simon Hugo
Design Manager Ron Stobbart
Publishing Manager Julie Ferris
Art Director Lisa Lanzarini
Publishing Director Simon Beecroft
Pre-Production Producer Marc Staples
Producer Louise Daly

Reading Consultant
Linda B. Gambrell, Ph.D.

First published in the United States in 2015 by DK Publishing
4th Floor, 345 Hudson Street, New York, New York 10014

10 9 8 7 6 5 4 3 2

002–273729–Feb/15

DK books are available at special discounts when purchased in bulk
for sales promotions, premiums, fund-raising, or educational use.
For details, contact:
DK Publishing Special Markets
4th Floor, 345 Hudson Street
New York, New York 10014
SpecialSales@dk.com

A catalog record for this book
is available from the Library of Congress.

ISBN: 978-1-4654-3011-3 (Paperback)
ISBN: 978-1-4654-3012-0 (Hardback)

Color reproduction by Altaimage UK
Printed and bound in China

www.dk.com
www.LEGO.com

A WORLD OF IDEAS:
SEE ALL THERE IS TO KNOW

Contents

Amazing Super Heroes

There are many Super Heroes in the universe. Some of the greatest heroes are Batman, Wonder Woman, and Superman.

They each have amazing abilities that help them in their quest to keep the world safe. The villains of the world had better watch out!

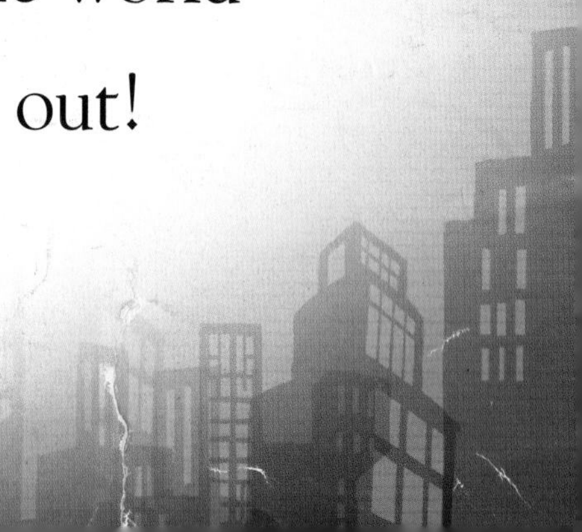

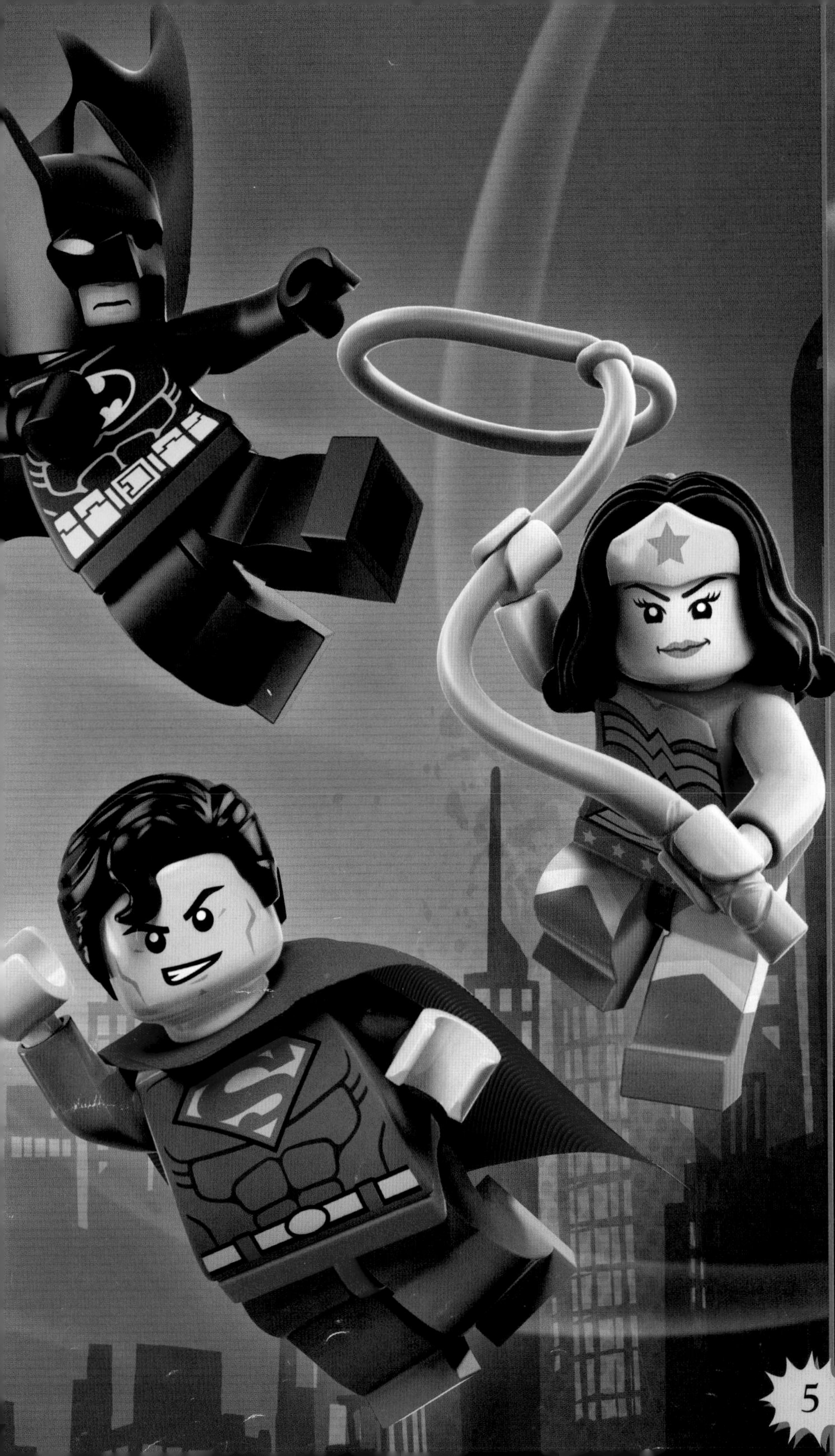

Superman

Superman comes from planet Krypton. Now he lives on planet Earth in the city of Metropolis.

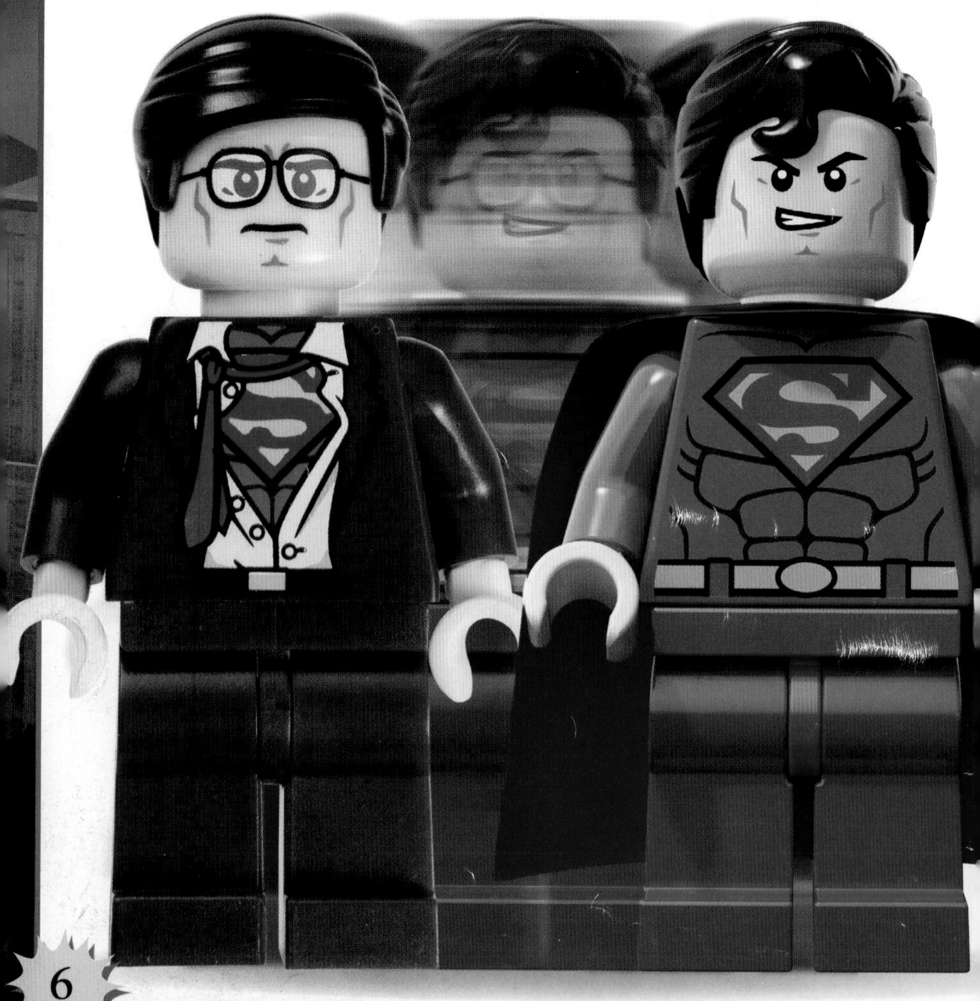

Superman hides his superpowers by having another identity. His other identity is a newspaper reporter named Clark Kent. No one knows that Superman and Clark Kent are secretly the same person.

Supergirl is another Super Hero from planet Krypton. She sometimes helps Superman on his missions.

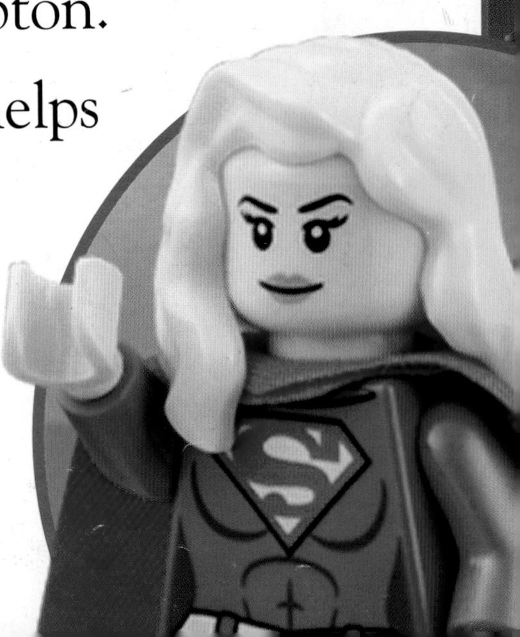

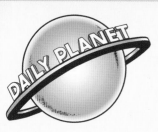

THE
DAILY

SUPER HEROES

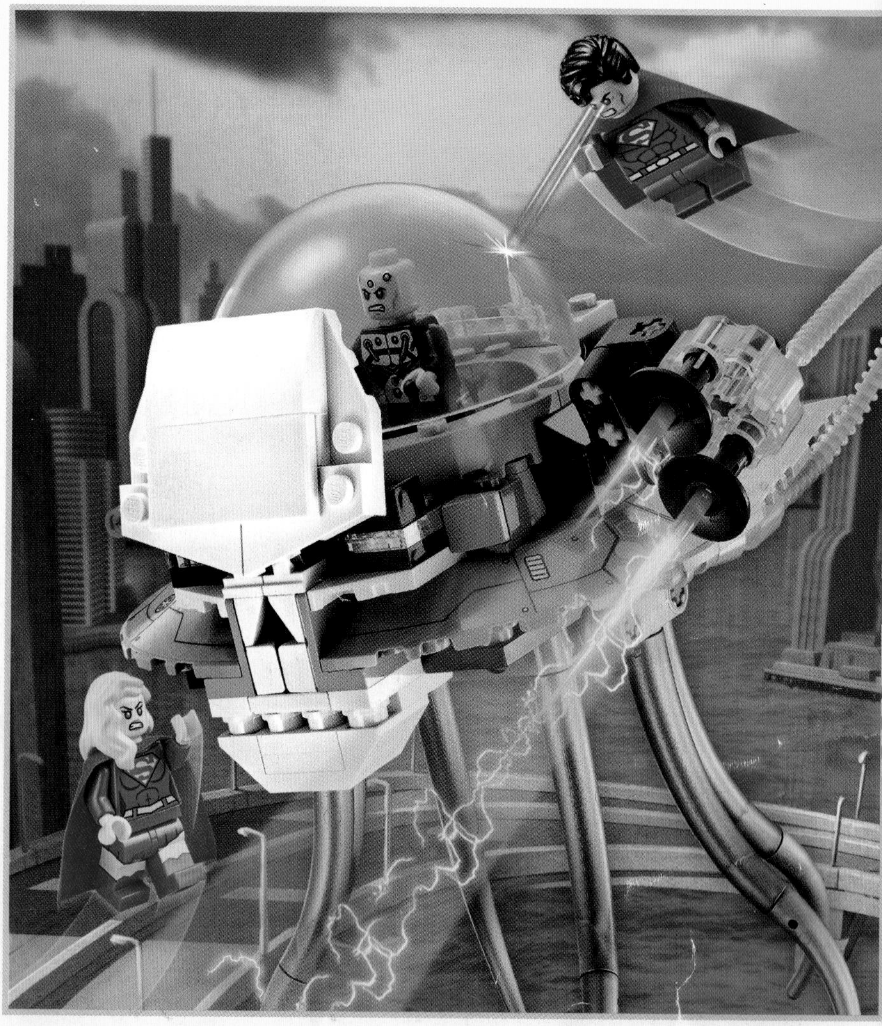

PLANET

SPECIAL EDITION

SAVE THE DAY

By Lois Lane

The mean, green villain known as Brainiac launched an attack on downtown Metropolis yesterday. Superman and Supergirl defeated the villain and saved our city.

Office worker Fred Jones saw Brainiac invade the city in his gigantic Skull Ship. Mr Jones told the *Daily Planet*, "The Skull Ship was tearing down buildings with its huge tentacles and destroying everything with its scary cannon. It's lucky that Superman and Supergirl were around to save us."

Witnesses saw Superman and Supergirl use their heat vision to destroy the Skull Ship.

This is the latest in a long line of daring rescues by Superman and Supergirl as they continue to keep our city safe.

Brave heroes, Superman and Supergirl

Trouble in Metropolis

Lois Lane is a journalist for the *Daily Planet* newspaper.

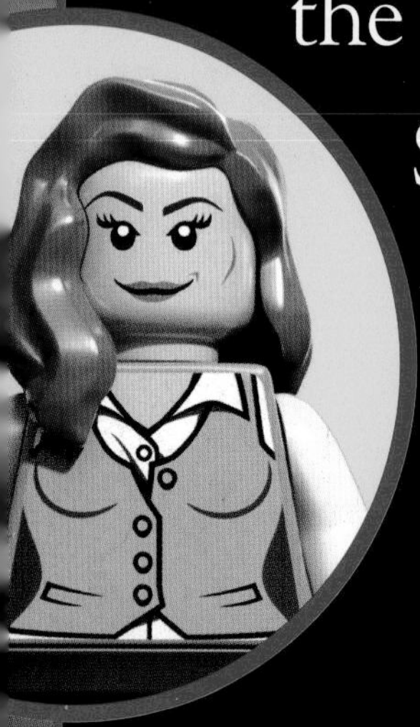

She writes news stories about Superman. Now she is about to become a news story herself!

General Zod, Faora, and Tor-An are villains from Krypton. They have hatched an evil plot to capture Lois in their Black Zero Dropship.

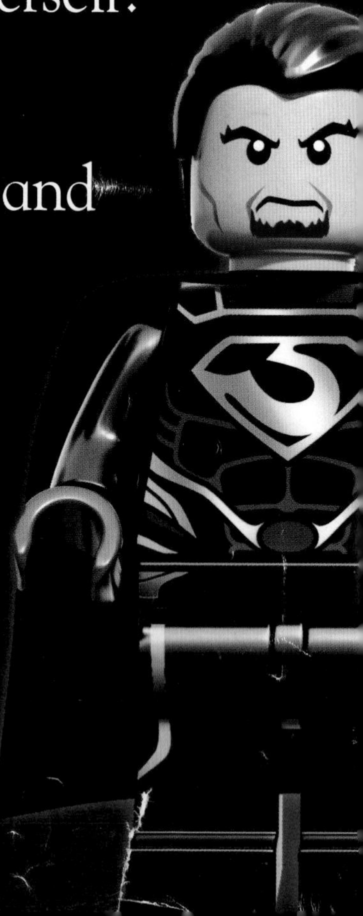

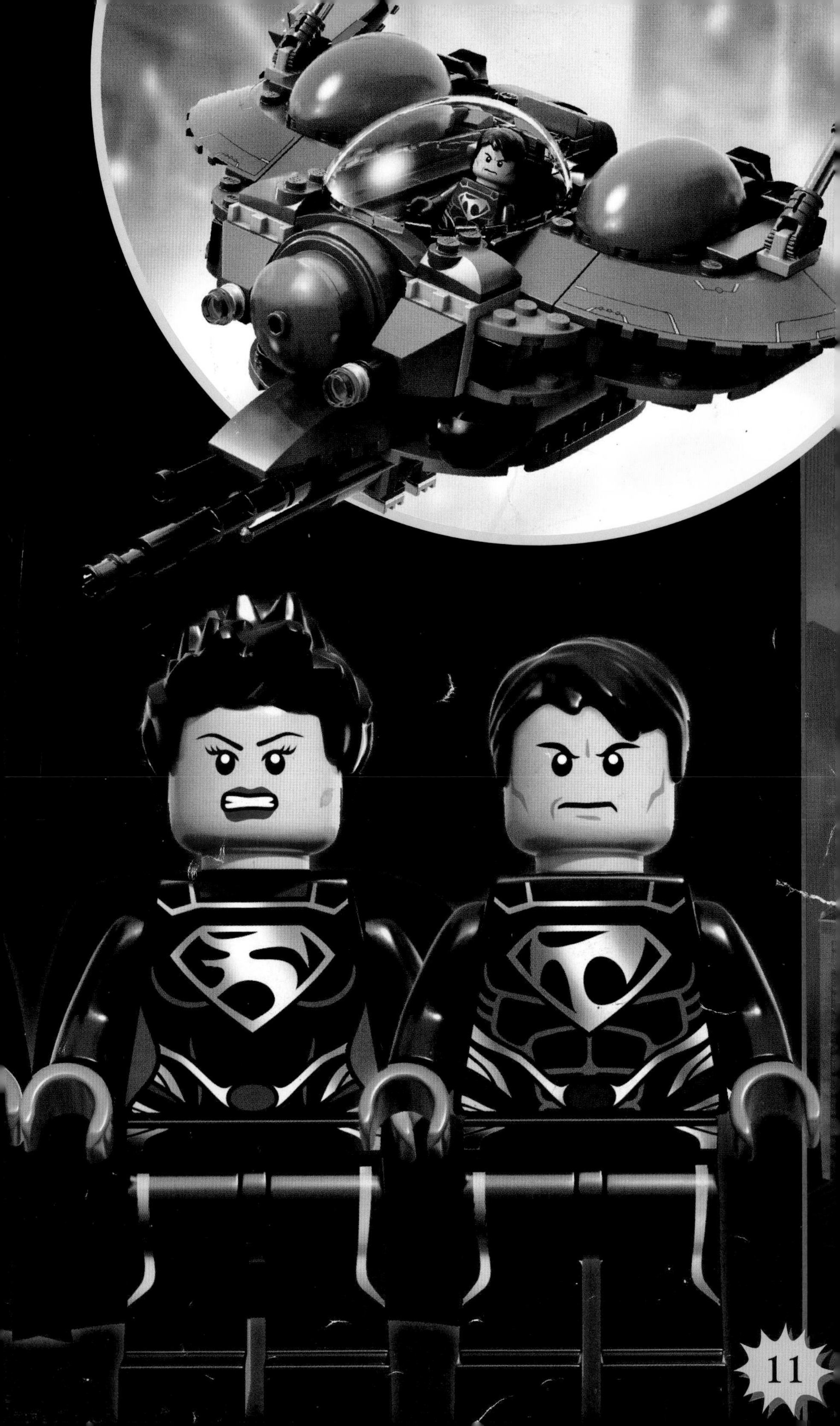

METROPOLIS POLICE DEPARTMENT

MOST WANTED

HOME   ABOUT US   NEWS

General Zod

Dangerous Villain

Description: Black hair, bushy eyebrows, angry expression.

Last seen wearing: A black cape and black armor with a silver emblem on his chest.

REWARD: $25,000

SEARCH

Contact us with information about a crime.

MOST WANTED REPORT A CRIME

Faora

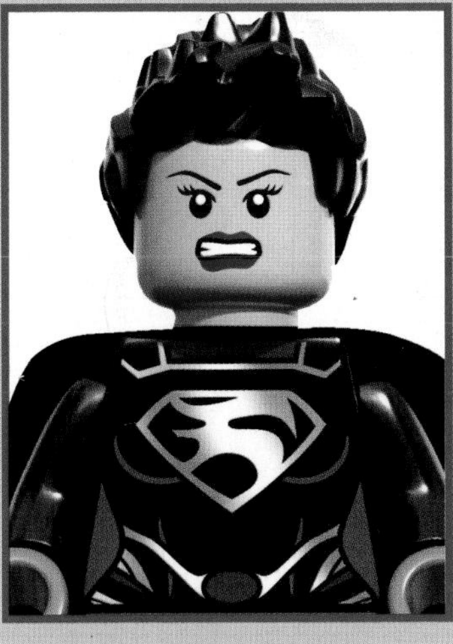

Evil Accomplice to General Zod

Description: Black hair, red lips, scary snarl.

Reward: $10,000

Tor-An

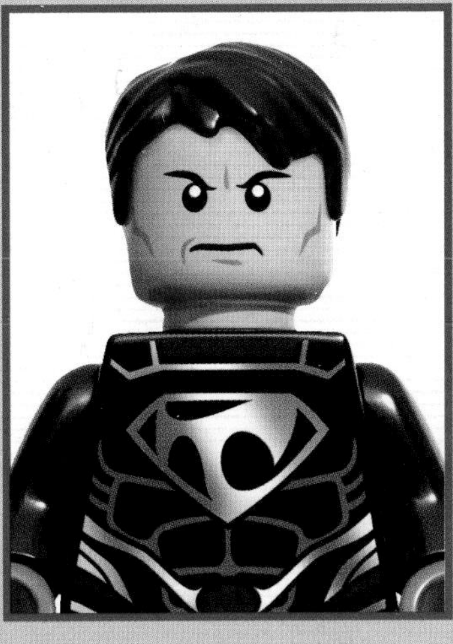

Evil Accomplice to General Zod

Description: Short brown hair, determined grimace.

Reward: $10,000

CLAIM REWARD

Metropolis Rescue

Superman is on a rescue mission! General Zod is holding Lois captive inside his Black Zero Dropship. Can Superman save her?

Superman flies onto the Black Zero Dropship. General Zod puts on his armor and fights Superman. While Superman is battling Zod, Lois runs to the ship's escape pod. She flees to safety, while Superman defeats Zod.

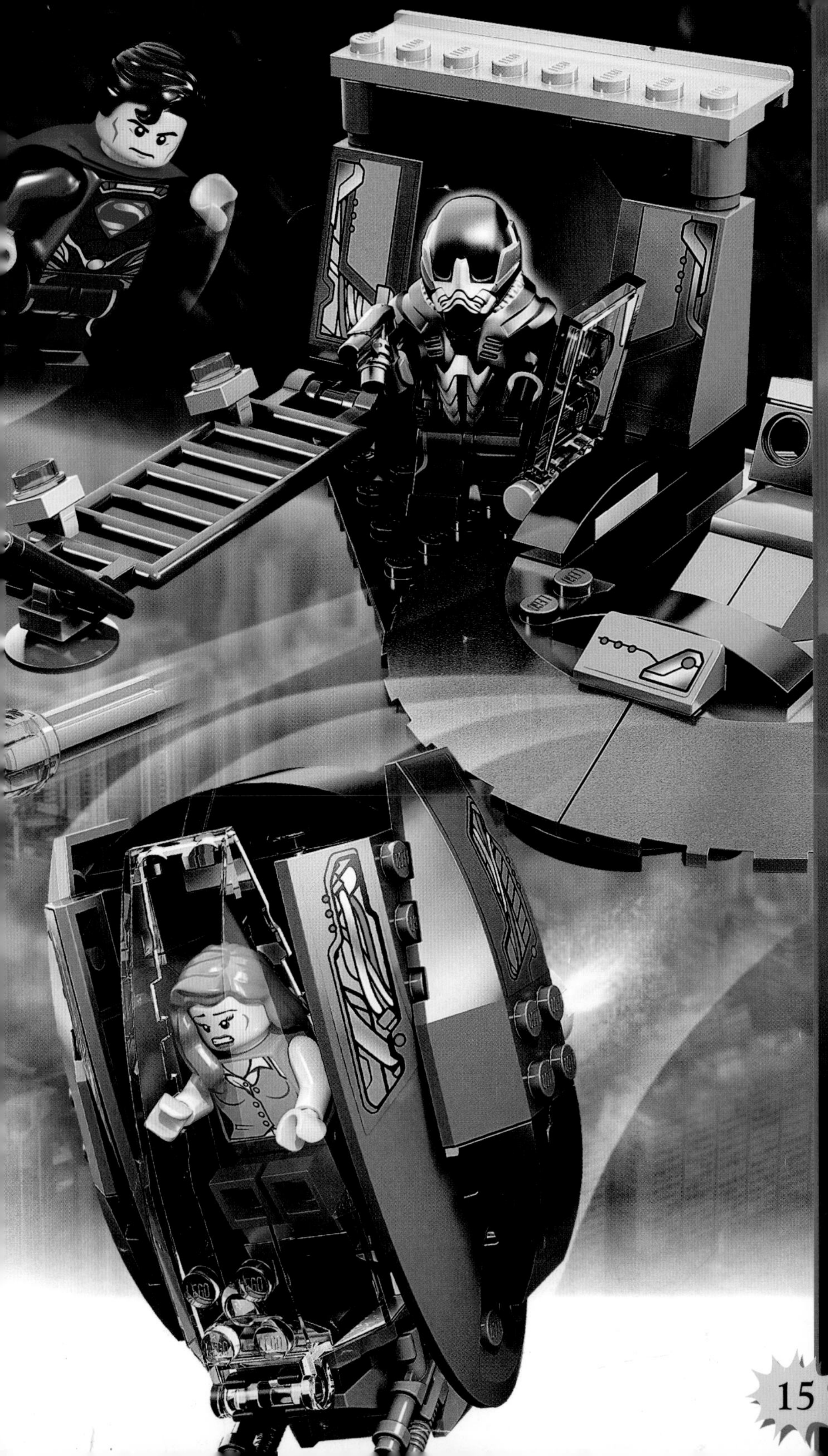

Batman

Batman's mission is to protect Gotham City from crime. He fights villains with special gadgets and martial arts skills.

Just like Superman, Batman has another identity. Most people know him as the rich businessman Bruce Wayne. At night, Bruce puts on the Batsuit and fights criminals as Batman.

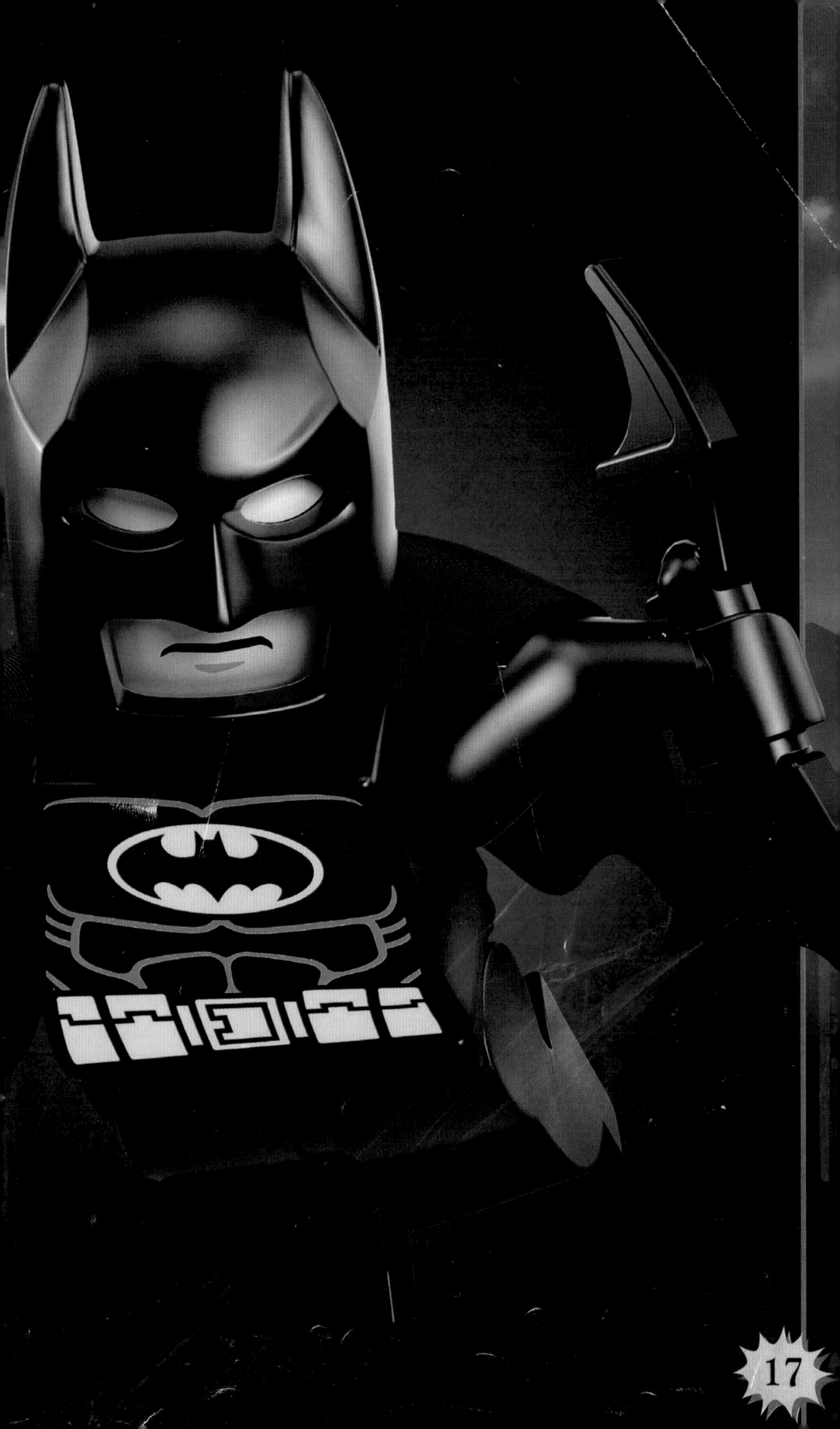

Batman's Gadgets

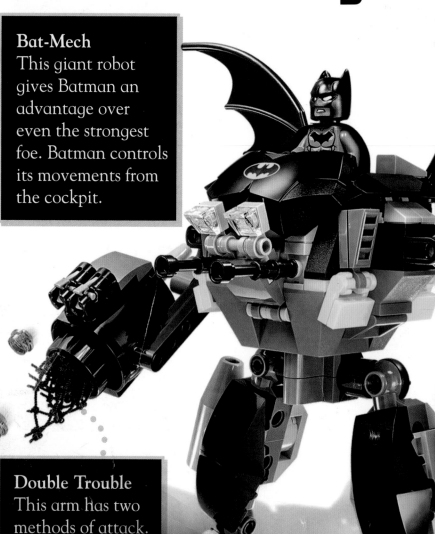

Bat-Mech
This giant robot gives Batman an advantage over even the strongest foe. Batman controls its movements from the cockpit.

Double Trouble
This arm has two methods of attack. Blasters fire powerful missiles, and a net shooter fires a net to trap enemies.

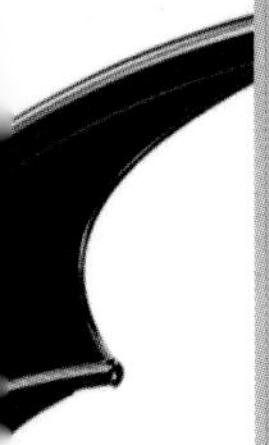

Batarangs
These weapons whizz through the air so Batman can knock out enemies from a distance.

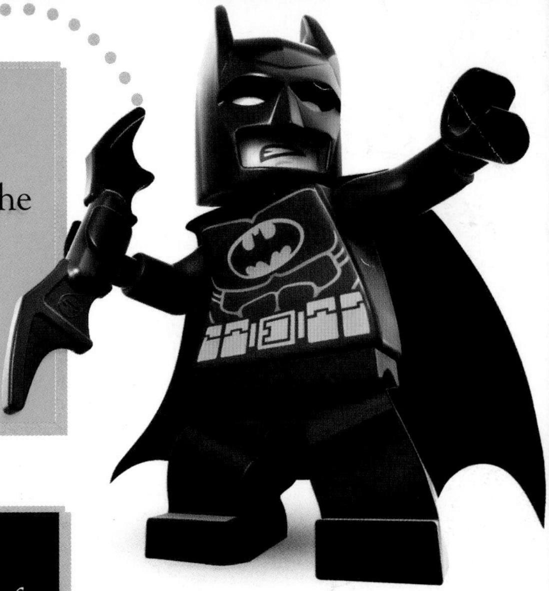

Robot Hand
The Bat-Mech's left arm has a flexible hand that can grab crooks. Handy!

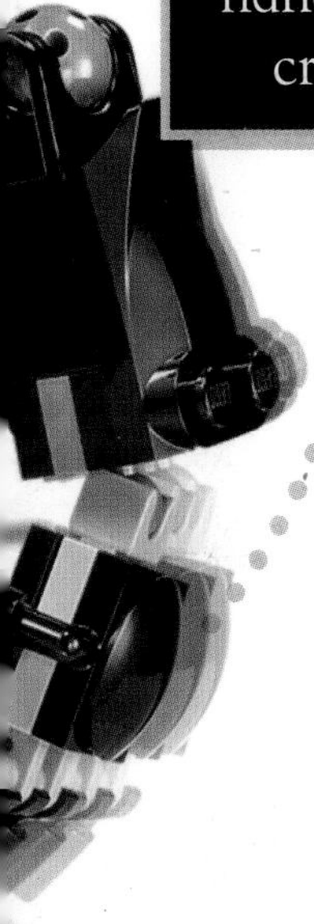

Breathing Apparatus
When Batman needs to chase enemies underwater, he wears this special tube so he can breathe.

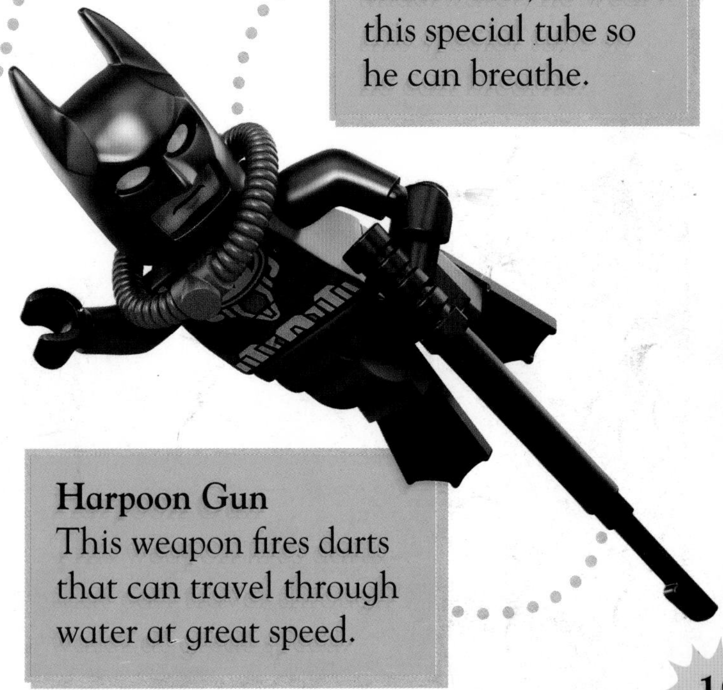

Harpoon Gun
This weapon fires darts that can travel through water at great speed.

The Joker

The Joker is one tricky criminal. He loves using wacky weapons to cause mayhem on the streets of Gotham City.

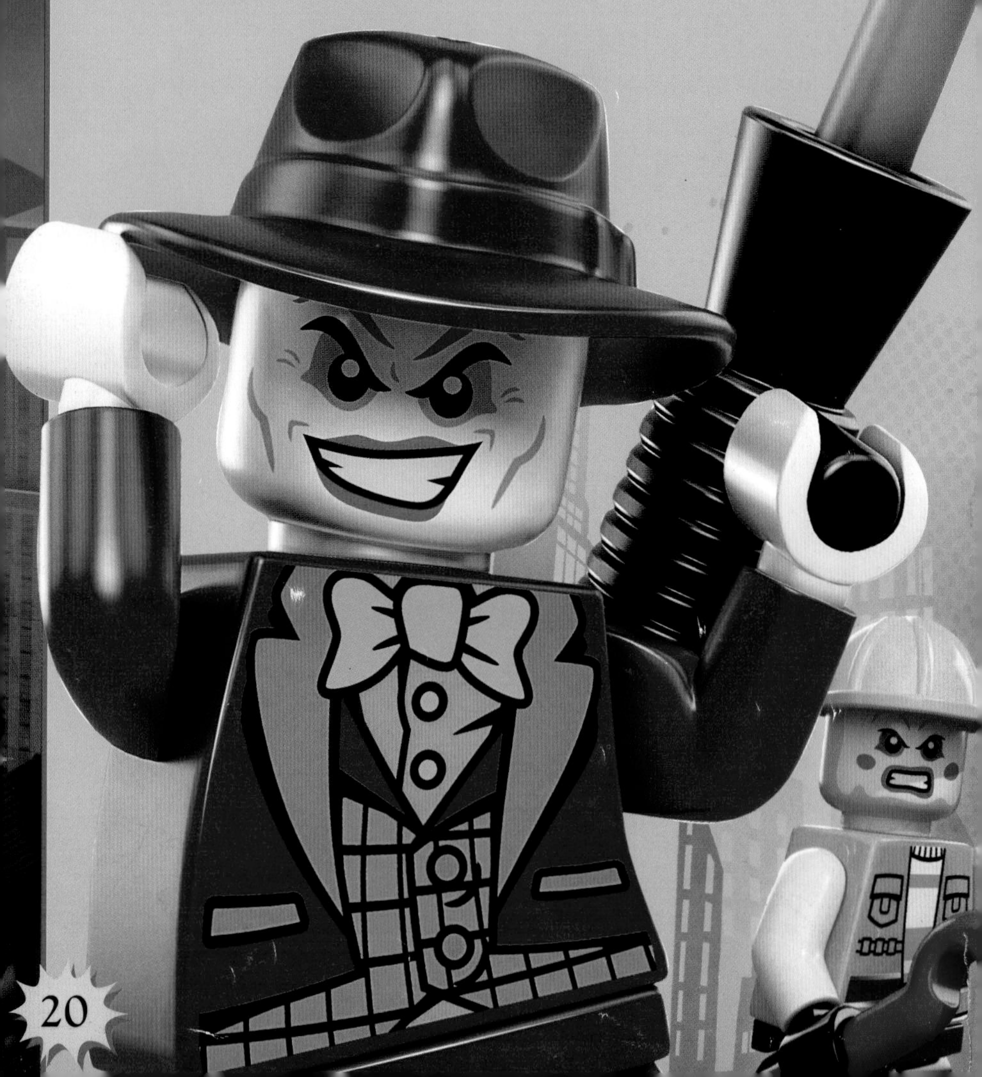

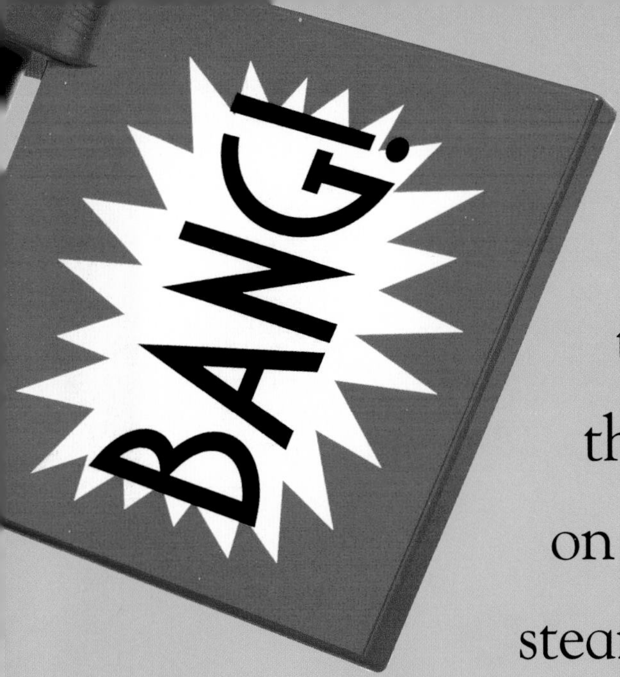
BANG!

He is
planning
to attack
the city
on a crazy
steamroller.

The Joker has lots of henchmen that help him carry out his schemes. He makes them wear clown face paint to match his own face. They are too scared of the Joker to argue!

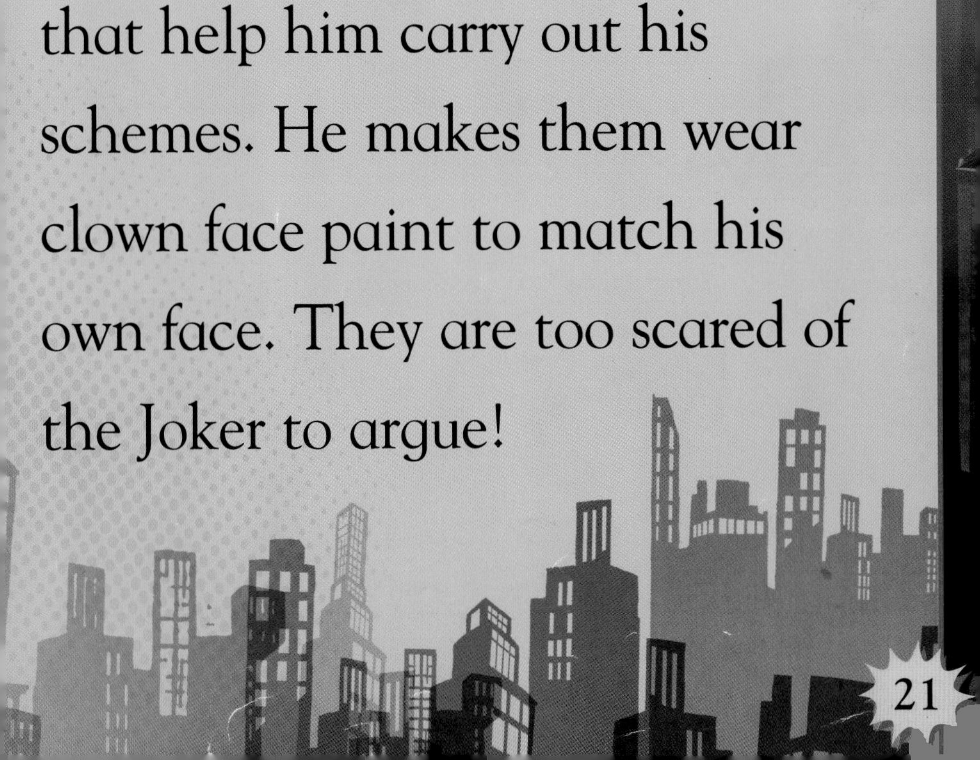

THE JOKER'S STEAMROLLER

THE JOKER HAS ADDED HIS OWN TWISTS TO THIS MENACING STEAMROLLER.

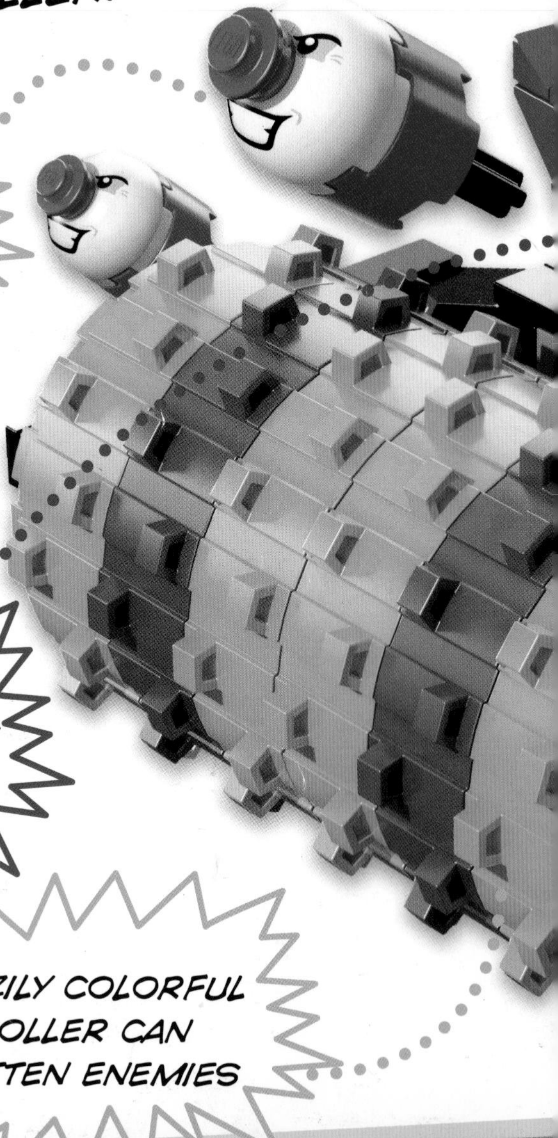

BOMBS FILLED WITH LAUGHING GAS

GRIN LOOKS LIKE THE JOKER'S INSANE SMILE

CRAZILY COLORFUL ROLLER CAN FLATTEN ENEMIES

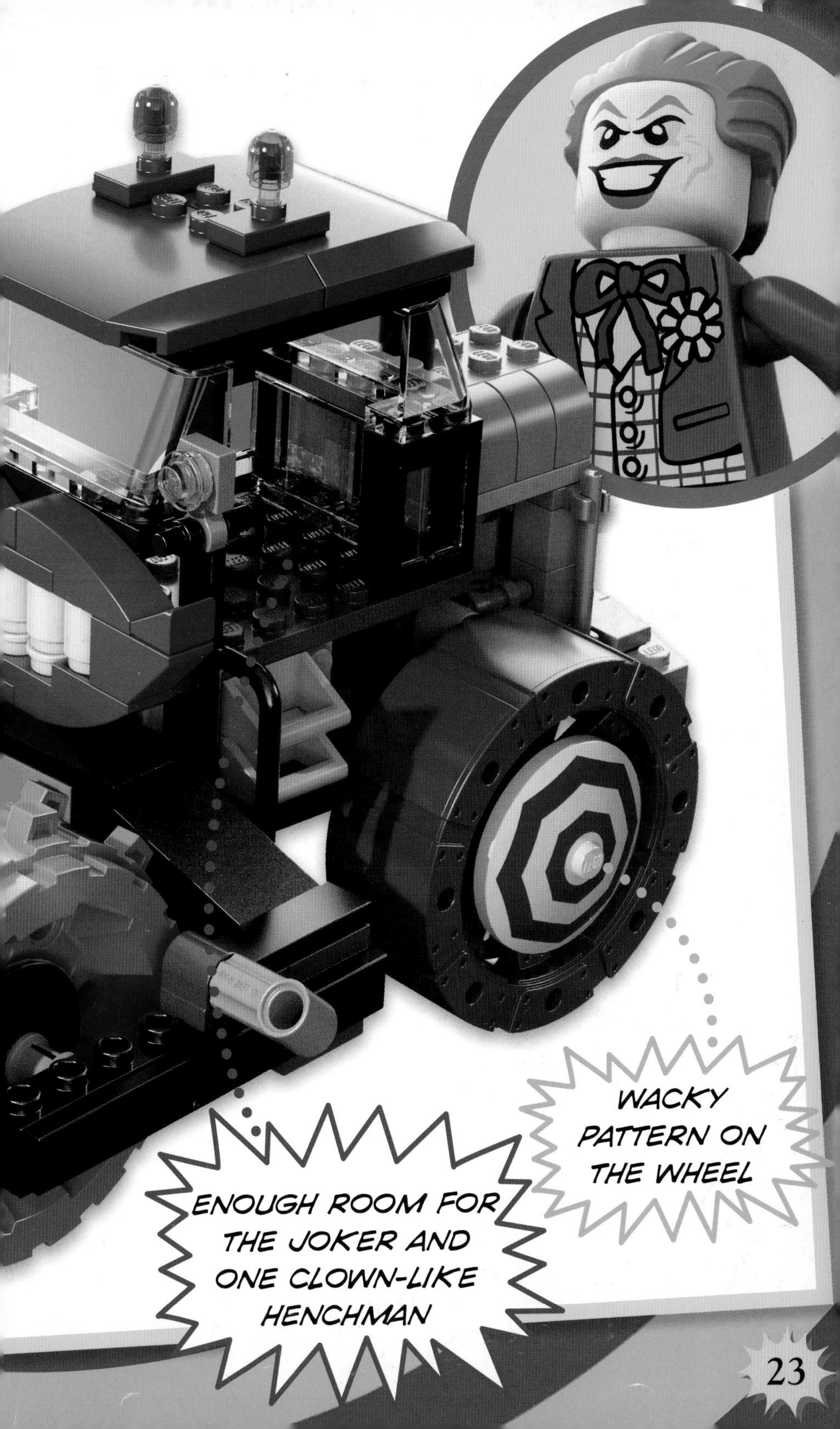
WACKY
PATTERN ON
THE WHEEL
ENOUGH ROOM FOR
THE JOKER AND
ONE CLOWN-LIKE
HENCHMAN

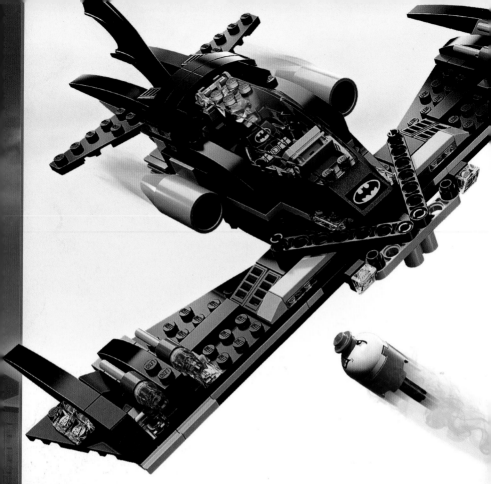

Battle for
Gotham City

Whoosh! Here comes Batman
in his speedy Batwing.
He is rushing to defend
Gotham City from the Joker.

The Joker is attacking the city on his scary steamroller. It is flattening everything in its path! The Joker fires laughing-gas bombs, but the Batwing dodges them. Batman swoops down to stop the steamroller in its tracks.

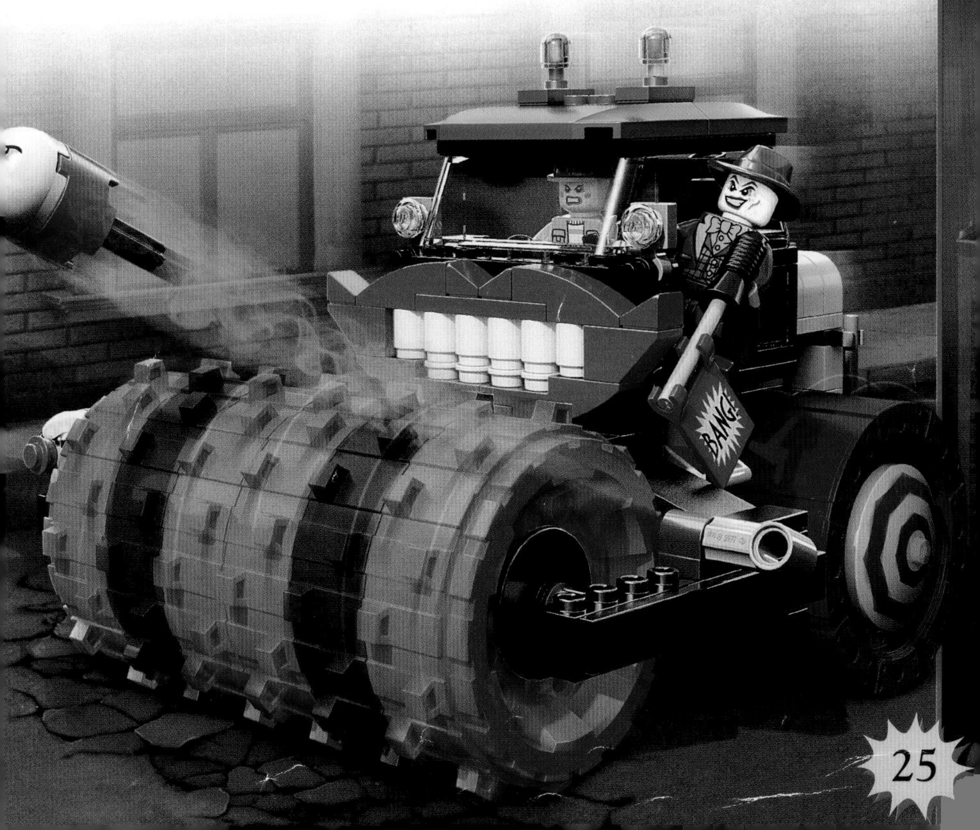
BANG!

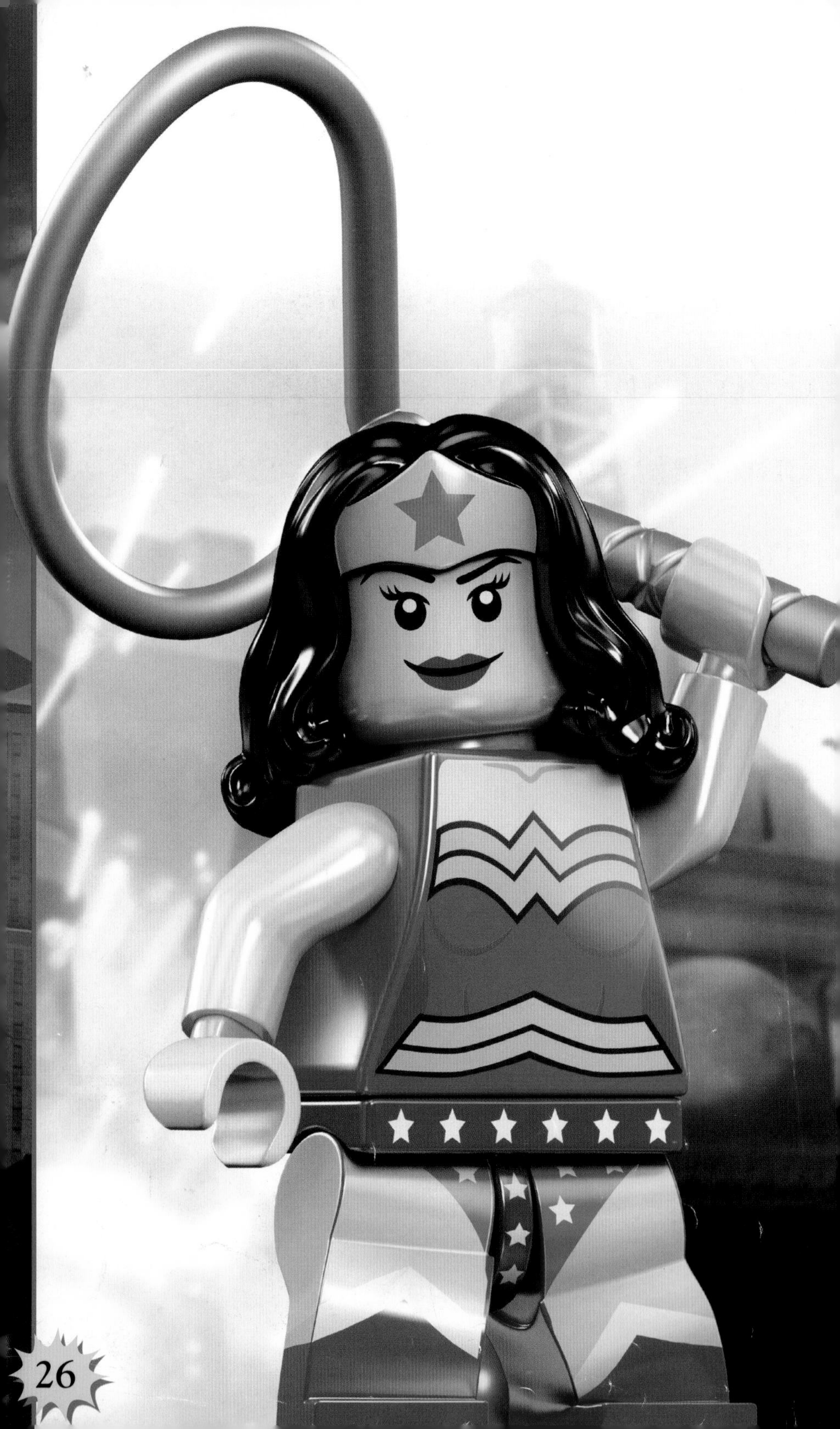

Wonder Woman

Wonder Woman has some special tools that help her defeat villains. When villains are caught in her Lasso of Truth, they confess their crimes.

Wonder Woman also has an Invisible Jet. Her Invisible Jet can't be seen by her enemies, so she can use it to sneak up on them.

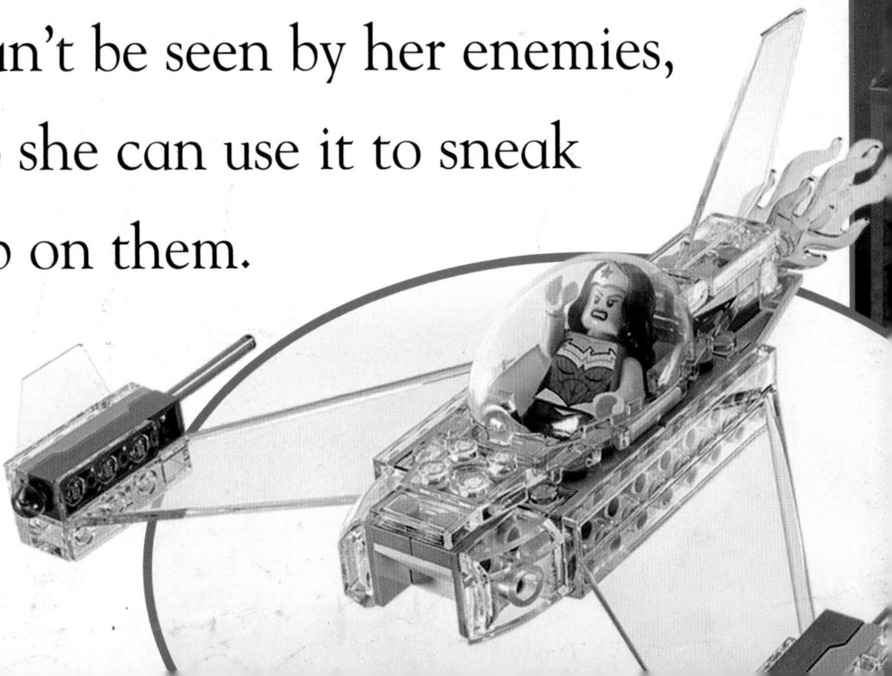

Heroes Unite

There is a terrifying new threat to the world's safety. A very strong and clever crook is planning a fiendish raid on Gotham City.

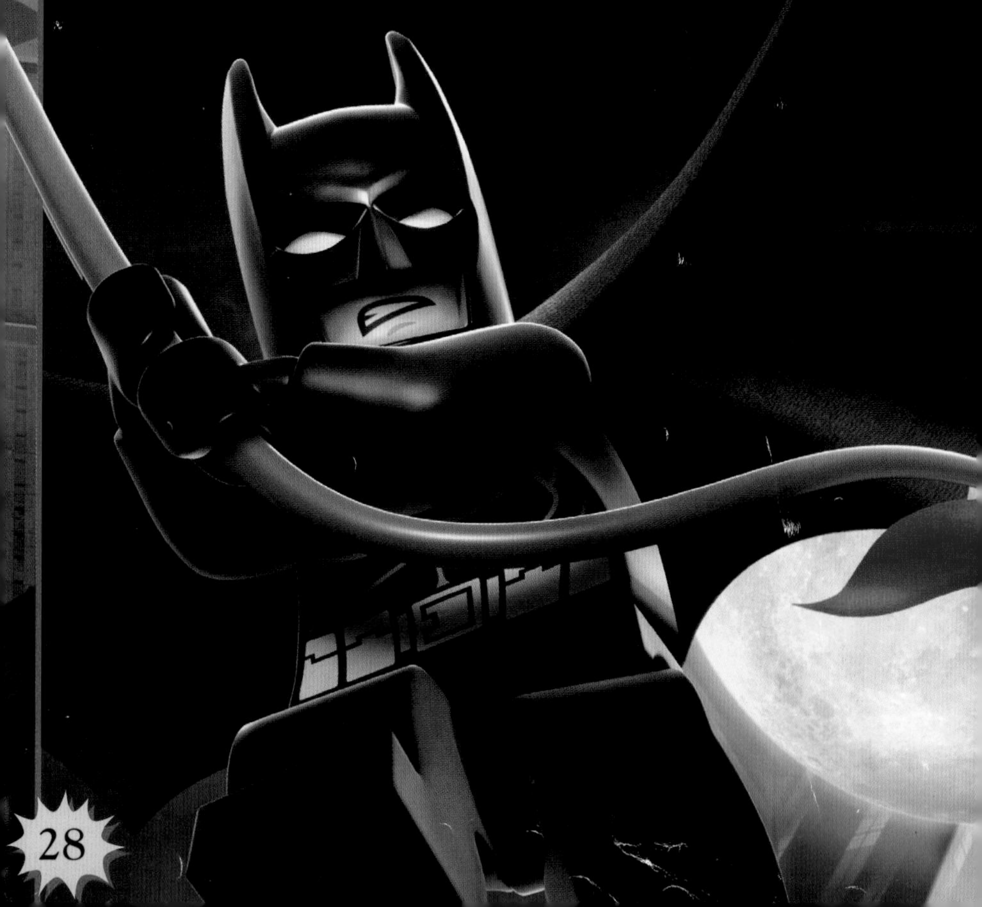

These Super Heroes
will need to work
together as a team
in order to put a stop
to this villain's
monkey business...

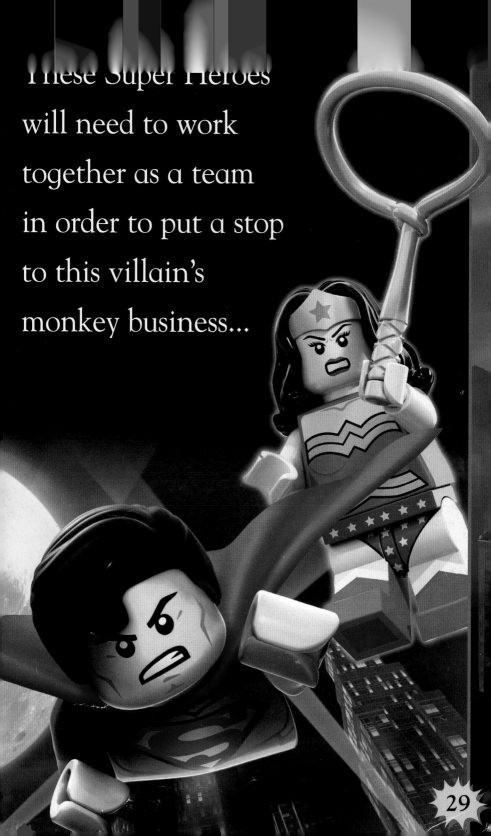

EMERGENCY CALL!

Calling all Super Heroes! There is another villain on the loose.

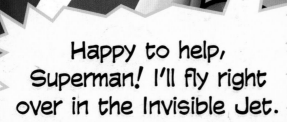

Happy to help, Superman! I'll fly right over in the Invisible Jet.

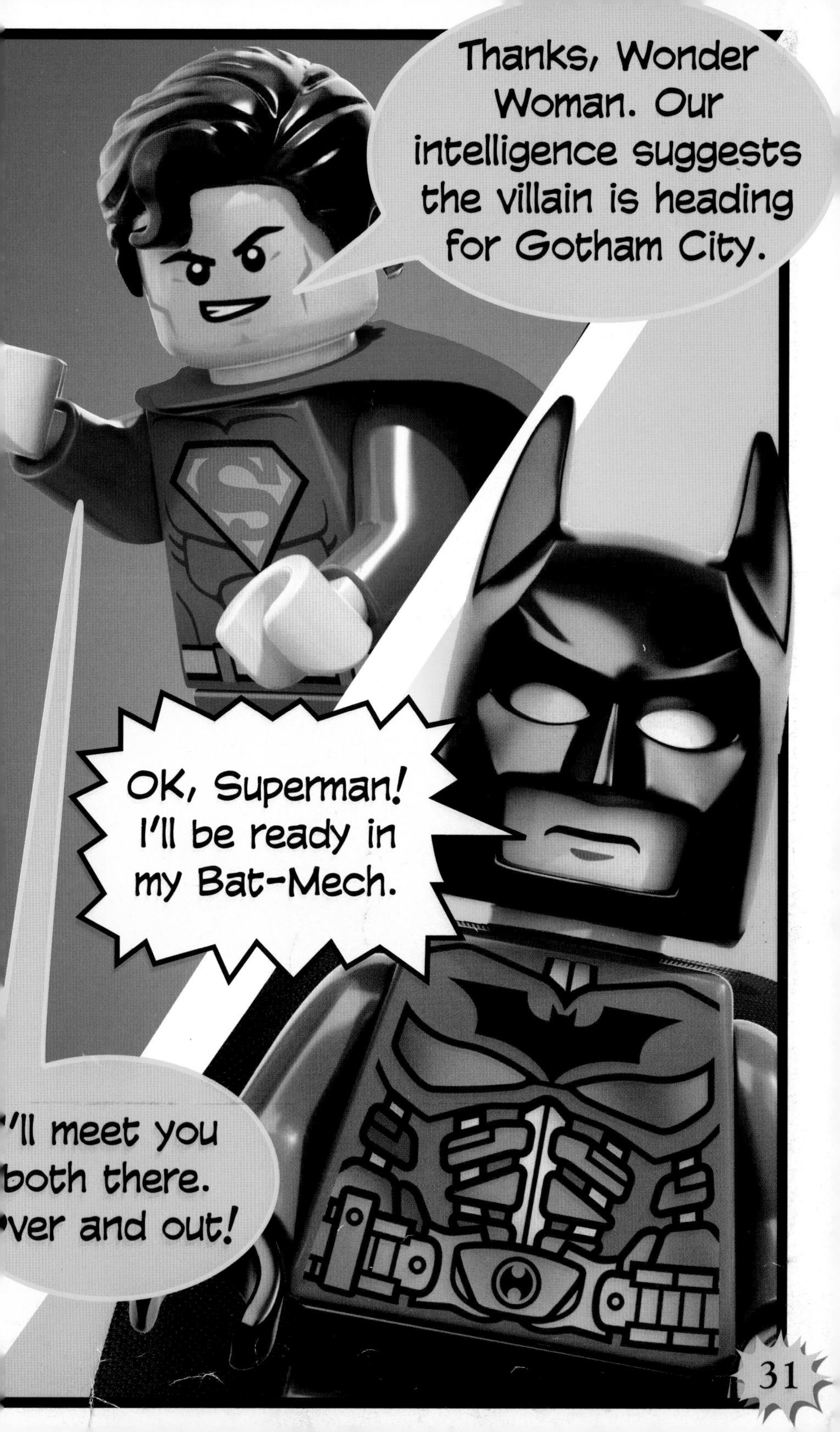
Thanks, Wonder Woman. Our intelligence suggests the villain is heading for Gotham City.
OK, Superman! I'll be ready in my Bat-Mech.
'll meet you both there. ver and out!

Gorilla Grodd

Gorilla Grodd is an evil gorilla. He is very intelligent, and is always thinking about his next wicked plot. He has even invented a special mind-control device that he wears on his head.

His latest plan is to attack Gotham City and steal the city's bananas. Gorilla Grodd loves bananas and will stop at nothing to get his hairy hands on them.

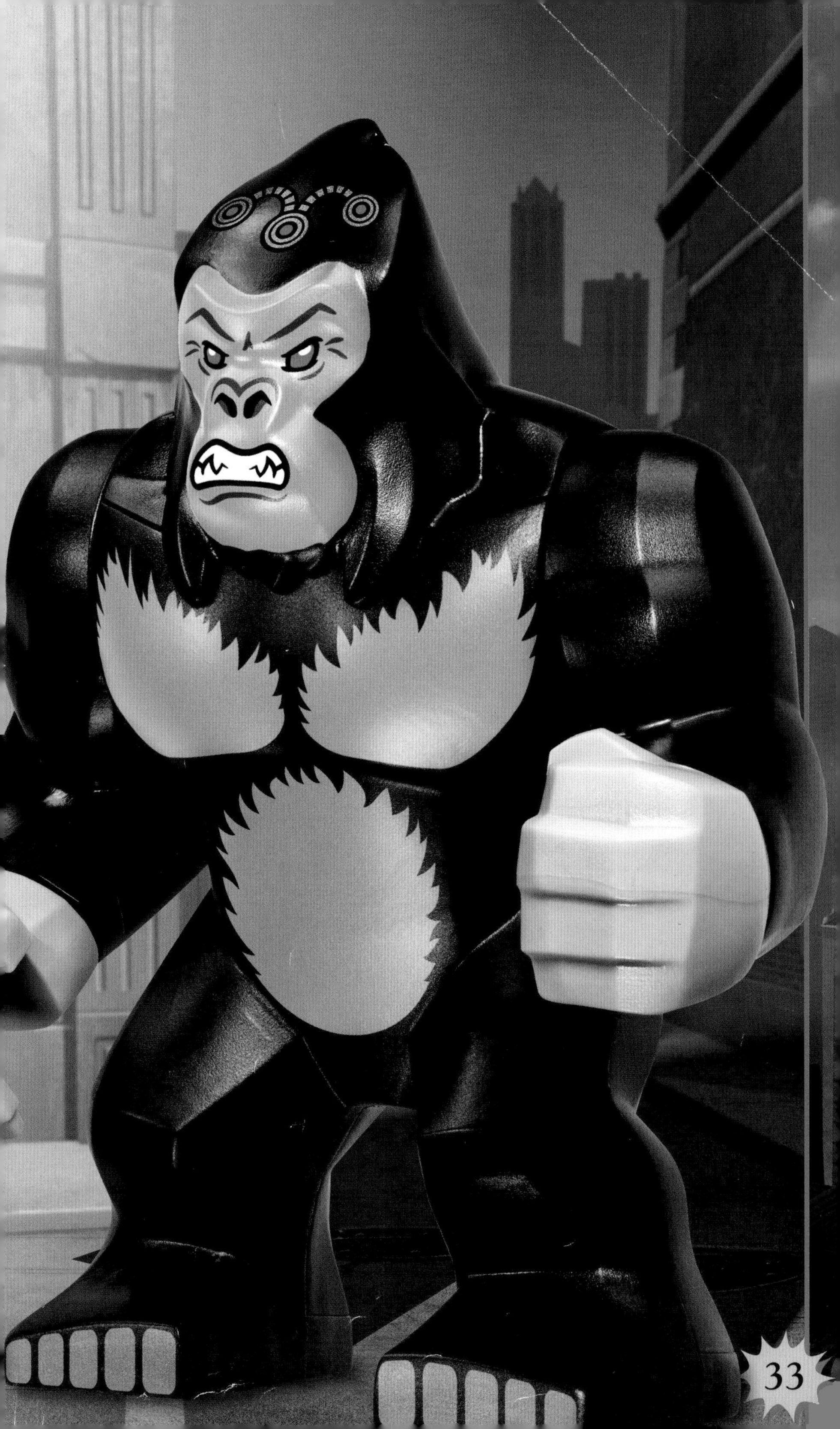

Inside the Mind of Gorilla Grodd

What thoughts cross the mind of an evil gorilla?

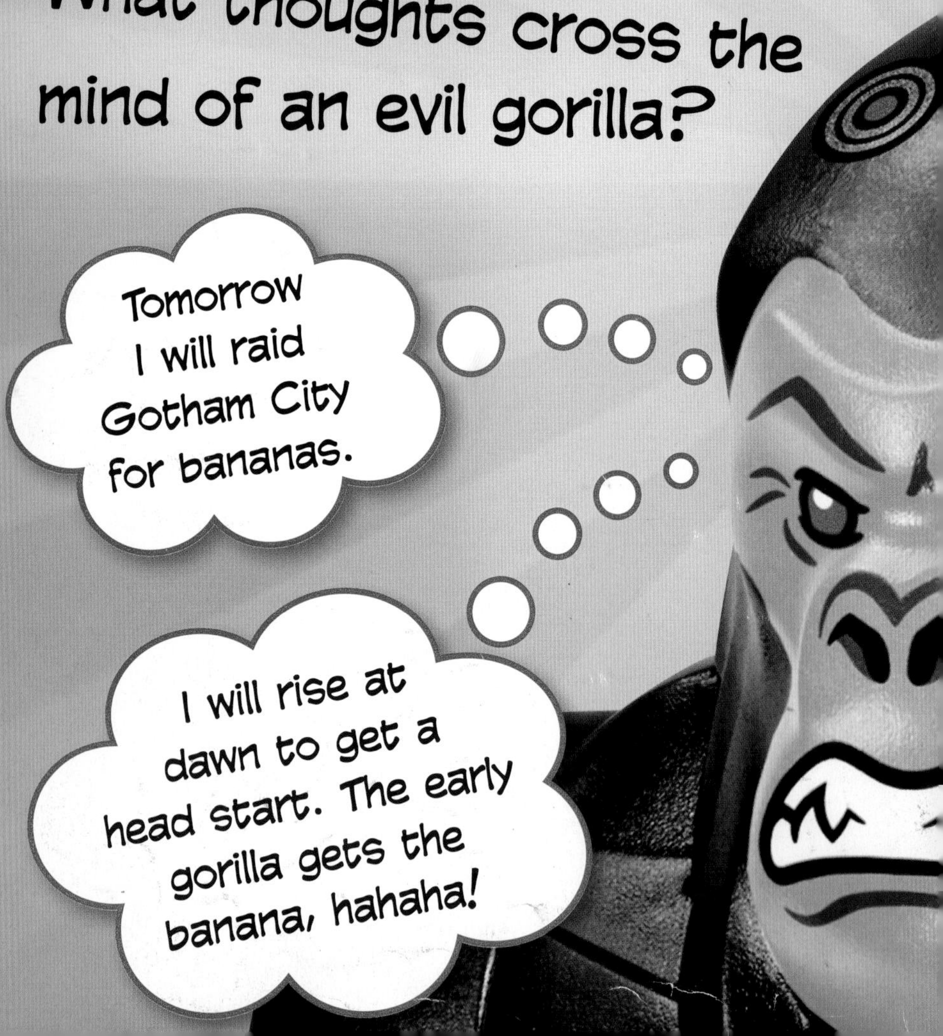
Tomorrow I will raid Gotham City for bananas.
I will rise at dawn to get a head start. The early gorilla gets the banana, hahaha!

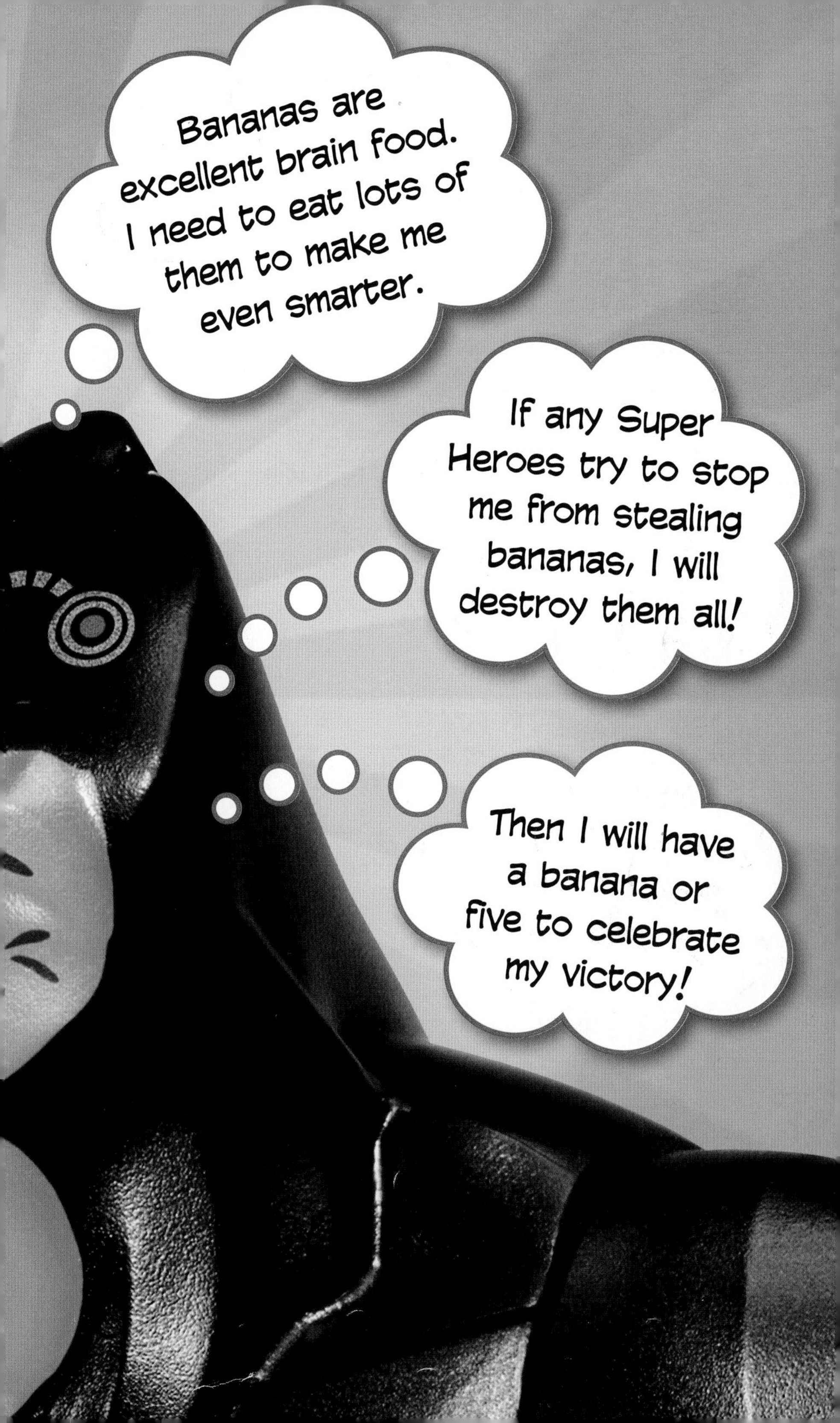
Bananas are excellent brain food. I need to eat lots of them to make me even smarter.
If any Super Heroes try to stop me from stealing bananas, I will destroy them all!
Then I will have a banana or five to celebrate my victory!

Banana Battle

Gorilla Grodd is feeling hungry!
He spots a banana delivery truck
and decides to steal bananas
from it. Greedy Grodd lifts the
truck into the air and shakes it,
sending the bananas flying.
The poor driver
is terrified!

Here comes Batman in his Bat-Mech! He stomps toward Grodd. Uh-oh! Watch out for that banana, Batman! The Bat-Mech slips and falls with a crash. Batman needs backup!

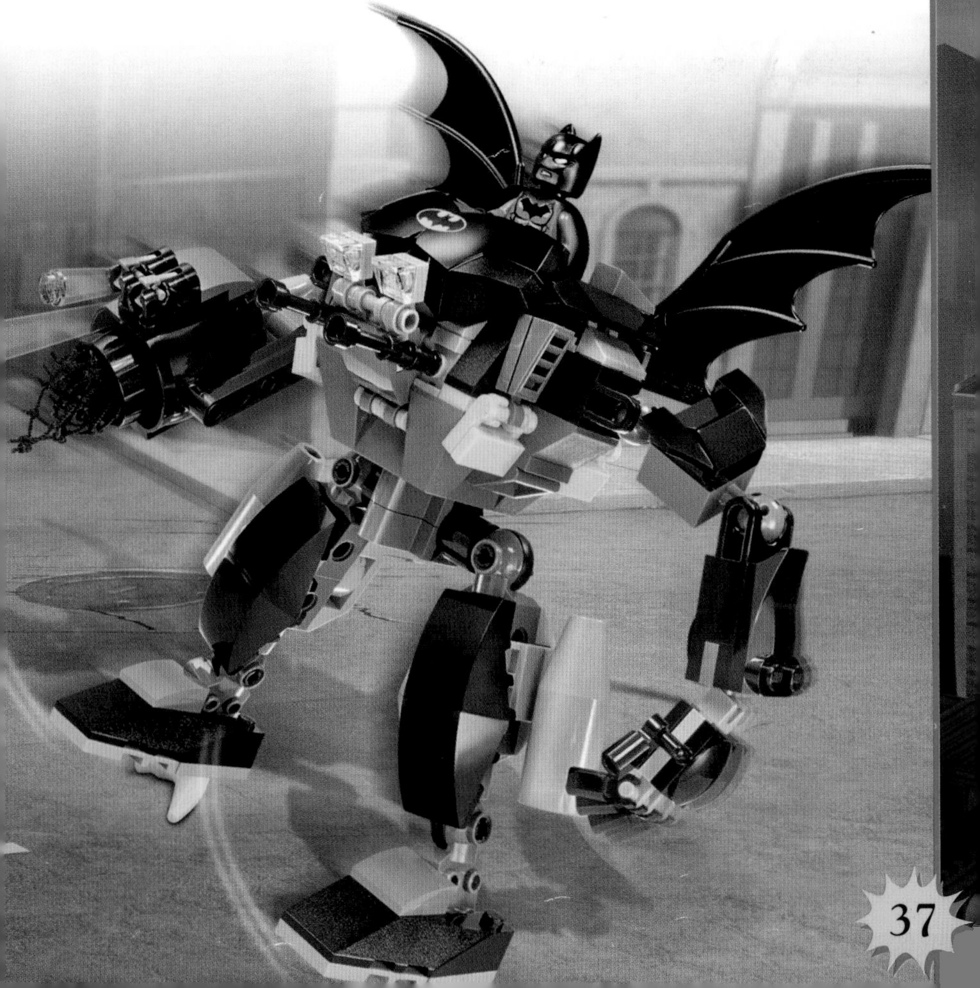

BANANA CO. GOTHAM CITY BRANCH

DRIVER'S DAILY LOG

All delivery activities must be logged daily by all drivers.

Banana Co.

DATE:	TIME:	NOTES:
Yesterday	*9.00am*	*Picked up bananas*
	10.00am	*Delivered bananas*
	11.00am	*Picked up bananas*
	Midday	*Delivered bananas*

DATE:	TIME:	NOTES:
Today	9.00am	Picked up bananas
	10.00am	Delivered bananas
	11.00am	Picked up bananas
	Midday	Attacked by an evil gorilla!

Super Heroes' Victory

Wonder Woman swoops in on her Invisible Jet. Gorilla Grodd can't see her! She takes aim and fires the jet's missiles at Grodd, taking him by surprise.

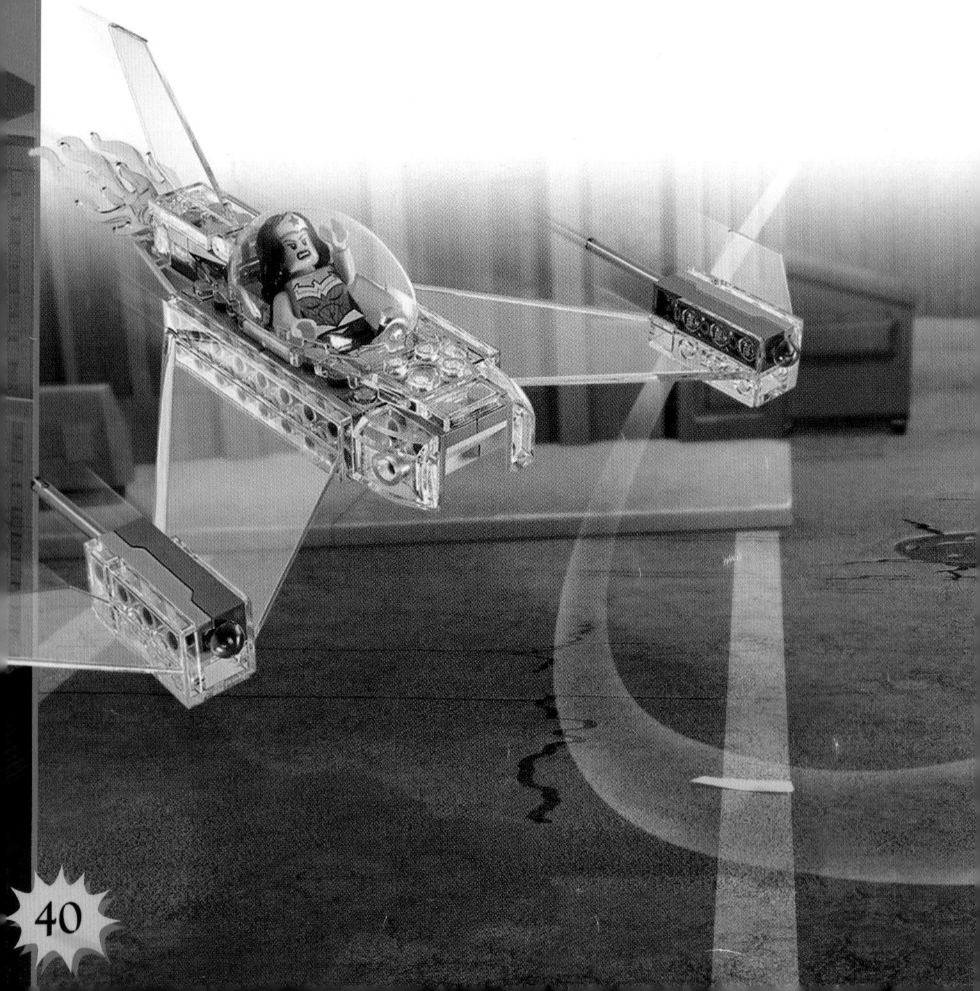

Next, Superman arrives and uses his super-strength to deliver a knockout blow to Gorilla Grodd. Grodd is finally defeated! The Super Heroes worked as a team to save the day. Good job, Super Heroes!

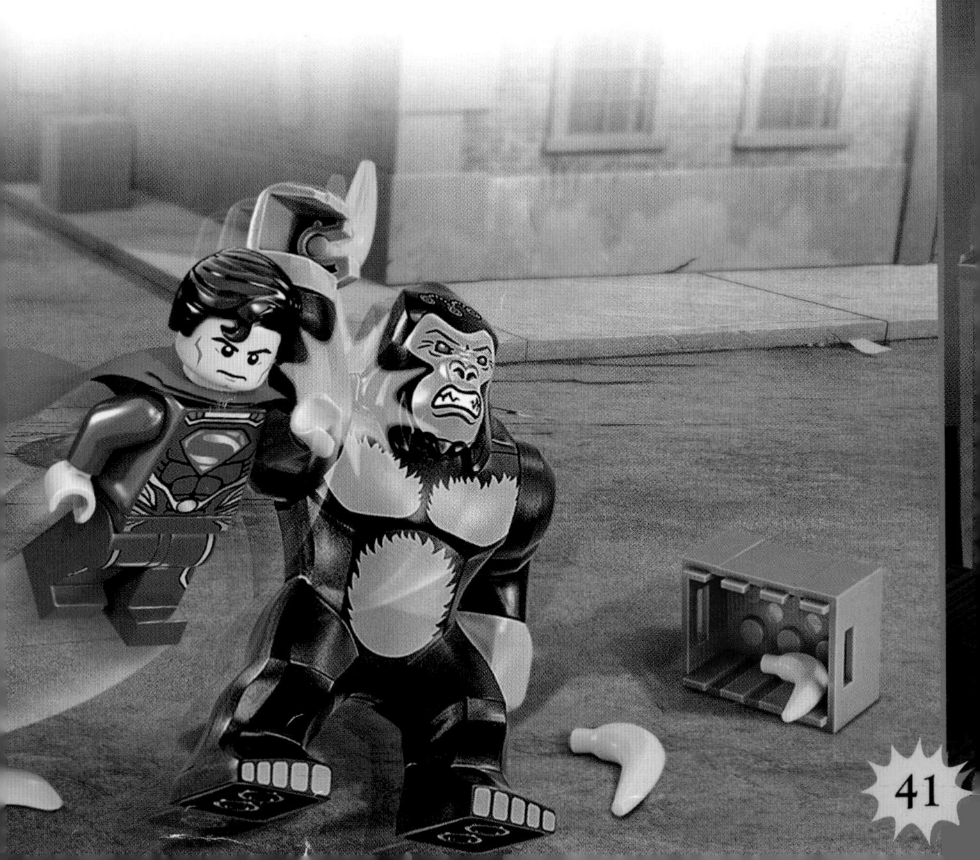

Quiz

1. Where does Superman live?

2. Which Super Hero uses special gadgets?

3. Which villain has a steamroller?

4. What does Gorilla Grodd like to eat?

5. What does Wonder Woman use to sneak past her enemies?

6. Where does General Zod hold Lois Lane captive?

7. Which Super Hero has a Lasso of Truth?

8. What is the name of Batman's other identity?

Answers on page 45.

Glossary

captive
unable to escape

confess
to tell the truth, or own up to something

fiendish
wicked and mean

gadgets
useful devices

invisible
can't be seen

intelligence
valuable information

journalist
someone who writes for a newspaper

martial arts
sports that teach fighting skills or self-defense

mayhem
a crazy, out of control situation

unite
join together

victory
a big win

Index

Answers to the quiz on pages 42 and 43:
1. Metropolis 2. Batman 3. The Joker 4. Bananas 5. Her Invisible Jet
6. The Black Zero Dropship 7. Wonder Woman 8. Bruce Wayne

Guide for Parents

DK Readers is a four-level interactive reading adventure series for children, developing the habit of reading widely for both pleasure and information. These books have an exciting main narrative interspersed with a range of reading genres to suit your child's reading ability, as required by the Common Core State Standards. Each book is designed to develop your child's reading skills, fluency, grammar awareness, and comprehension in order to build confidence and engagement when reading.

Ready for a *Beginning to Read Alone* book
YOUR CHILD SHOULD

- be able to read many words without needing to stop and break them down into sound parts.
- read smoothly, in phrases and with expression.
  By this level, your child will be beginning to read silently.
- self-correct when a word or sentence doesn't sound right.

A Valuable and Shared Reading Experience

For some children, text reading, particularly non-fiction, requires much effort, but adult participation can make this both fun and easier. So here are a few tips on how to use this book with your child.

TIP 1 Check out the contents together before your child begins:
- invite your child to check the blurb, contents page, and layout of the book and comment on it.
- ask your child to make predictions about the story.
- talk about the information your child might want to find out.

TIP 2 Encourage fluent and flexible reading:
- support your child to read in fluent, expressive phrases, making full use of punctuation and thinking about the meaning.

- help your child learn to read with expression by choosing a sentence to read aloud and demonstrating how to do this.

TIP 3 Indicators that your child is reading for meaning:

- your child will be responding to the text if he/she is self-correcting and varying his/her voice.
- your child will want to talk about what he/she is reading or is eager to turn the page to find out what will happen next.

TIP 4 Chat at the end of each chapter:

- encourage your child to recall specific details after each chapter.
- let your child pick out interesting words and discuss what they mean.
- talk about what each of you found most interesting or most important.
- ask questions about the text. These help to develop comprehension skills and awareness of the language used.

A FEW ADDITIONAL TIPS

- Read to your child regularly to demonstrate fluency, phrasing, and expression; to find out or check information; and for sharing enjoyment.
- Encourage your child to reread favorite texts to increase reading confidence and fluency.
- Check that your child is reading a range of different types of material, such as jokes, and following instructions.

Series consultant, **Dr. Linda Gambrell**, Distinguished Professor of Education at Clement University, has served as President of the National Reading Conference, the College Reading Association, and the International Reading Association. She is also a reading consultant for the **DK Adventures** series.

Have you read these other great books from DK?

2

DK READERS
BEGINNING 2 TO READ ALONE
LEGO
THE LEGO MOVIE
AWESOME ADVENTURES
HELEN MURRAY

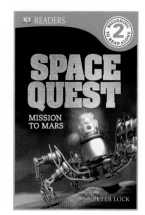

Meet Emmet and join him on his quest to save the universe!

DK READERS
BEGINNING 2 TO READ ALONE
LEGO
STAR WARS
THE EMPIRE STRIKES BACK

Can brave Luke Skywalker defeat sinister Darth Vader?

DK READERS
BEGINNING 2 TO READ ALONE
SPACE QUEST
MISSION TO MARS
PETER LOCK

Embark on a mission to explore the solar system. First stop—Mars.

3

DK Readers 3
LEGO
LEGENDS OF CHIMA
POWER UP!
Julia March

Discover the new tribes threatening Chima™ with their icy powers.

DK Readers 3
Hope for the Elephants
Patricia J. Murphy

Join David on an amazing trip to meet elephants in Asia and Africa.

DK Readers 3
LEGO
DC COMICS
SUPER HEROES
BATMAN'S MISSIONS
Beth Davies

Follow Batman as he fights to protect Gotham City from crime.

4/16